Race-Baiting
In
America

How The Left Use Race As A Means
To Keep Power, Drive The Narrative,
& Tear This Country Apart

D. Lee

ISBN: 1479147788
ISBN-13: 9781479147786

First Publishing: October, 2012

To contact the author for copies of the book or for appearances
or speaking engagements, please contact
author.dlee@gmail.com

Share With Your Family And Friends

This book is highly important to share with everyone you know. The main stream media should be giving lots of press to things like what I detail in this book, but they are not. Help to inform your fellow Americans about what is going on and how they can help stop it. I thank you for reading this book and for telling others about it.

~D. Lee
Email: author.dlee@gmail.com

Acknowledgments

This book came about because I became fed up with the ridiculous accusations that I had been hearing from left-leaning media outlets. Finally, I decided to take matters into my own hands, and the idea for this book was born.

Too often, we as Americans like to hope that some of the things that we hear just can't be true. And even if they are, we tell ourselves that it must be a fluke, an aberration, something that will not be heard again. We rely on the internal compass that most good folks have, or their close friends or family who will gently tell them of their misguided words. Sadly, in some folks the compass is badly misaligned, and the people closest to them either can't or won't use their influence.

I want to thank a number of folks who have helped this book come to pass. Because of the nature of this book and how it will be received in certain circles, I will not be naming them here; they do not deserve to be singled out for persecution. Just know that you good folks who have helped with this book, in big ways and small, are to be commended for your honesty and foresight, and I hope that with your help, this book will effect change in America.

I also want to thank you, the reader, for daring to pick this book up and to learn the truth about how the Left treats those that it disagrees with. My hope is that you will open your mind to what is going on and how it is shaping politics in America today. You are fearless for choosing to read this book, and hopefully you will continue to be fearless in not only sharing this book, but to begin to be more vocal in speaking out against what I detail on the pages herein.

~D. Lee
September 2012

Table of Contents

"Racism is man's gravest threat to man - the maximum of hatred for a minimum of reason."

~Abraham J. Heschel
Jewish theologian and philosopher, 1907-1972

INTRODUCTION

America. Land of the free, home of the brave. And also home to the race-baiting Left, who like to pigeon-hole Republicans and conservatives as racially backward rednecks who just can't help themselves from using racial language. I find this very troubling, especially in light of the fact that just a few years ago, America voted in the first black President in its history.

If racism is so bad, so prevalent (which it must be if Republicans just fling out racial comments on a daily basis), then how did we elect Barack Obama as President? One would think, listening to people at the *Huffington Post*, *New York Times*, *MSNBC*, *CNN* and a host of other news/media outlets, that Republicans, and especially the Tea Party, would have been able to mount a defense good enough to keep him from being elected. As the election results show, Obama received quite a bit of help from "white America".

Just how much of the country is made up of black people? Roughly 12.5%, depending on who does the research. That equals 37-38 million people. It's a lot, for sure, but is that total population enough to have gotten Obama elected? Hardly. The results of the election tell us just how many votes he received from the population: 69.5 million. That means that even if every black person in this country voted - women, men, the elderly, babies, teenagers, young adults, etc. - it would only account for slightly over half of the votes he garnered in 2008. So who were the other voters that helped to elect Obama? You guessed it: white people.

Lots of people like to say that blacks supported Obama in super-high numbers. I have no doubt that's true, but it still means that he needed plenty of other people who were not black to support him. Perhaps some of those votes were to prove to someone that they weren't racist. A pretty poor excuse to vote for someone, but I can understand that some folks need to maintain the Politically Correct narrative. Others voted for him because they actually like his positions. These are scarier folks, because they truly don't understand America, both as a country and as a concept. But regardless of the reason, the fact remains that Obama received a large number of white votes in order to win.

Look, let's be honest here. There are still some folks out there that truly do not like black people, or Hispanic people, or Asian people, or fill-in-the-blank people. Fine, let them be jerks. But the vast majority of us have moved on and discovered that when it gets down to it, there really is no such thing as race; it's a made-up word that people use as a means to divide people in order to better control them. Stop it! We're all people, end of story.

What I've put together is just a tiny bit of what is going on with folks from the Left. As I was researching them, I came to realize that in some of these cases, I had EXPECTED Democrats to use race as a means of attack because they've been doing so for quite some time. Yet some of these stories shocked me with just how blatant they were with using the issue of race in attacking the Right. And more than one of them had complete fabrications that were used in an attempt to prove racism by a Republican. The examples include TV personalities, elected officials, prominent leaders and others. It's crazy, and it's true. Read on for these incredible stories of race baiting, and tell me that it's all in my head.

Part 1:
The Handbook of Racial Code Words
(As Compiled By Michelle Malkin,
Commentary And Additions By D. Lee)

The Handbook Of Racial Code Words

I bet you didn't think that there was such a thing as a "handbook of racial code words", did you? Neither did I. But one enterprising conservative woman has compiled this information for us, and I think it deserves to be mentioned here, ahead of all of the examples that I will lay out for you later in this book. Michelle Malkin deserves the credit on getting this handbook started, and it probably never would have come together if not for the whole of the Left, especially those in the "mainstream media" who apparently have their "race radar" going at all times. They provided us with the insight in all of this race-baiting that is supposedly going on by the Right. Too bad they don't see that this is really coming from their own side. But, because we conservatives care about people, and don't want to offend anyone, I present *The Handbook of Racial Code Words*.

#1: Angry

Angry used to just mean that: angry. Not anymore. Apparently, this is racial coding that conservatives use to dredge up the notion of "the angry black man". As Michelle Malkin explains:

"You notice he said 'anger' twice," Touré fumed in response to a speech last week by GOP Presidential candidate Mitt Romney. "He's really trying to use racial coding and access some really deep stereotypes about the angry black man." Or maybe Romney is just accurately describing the singular temperament of the growling, finger-jabbing, failure-plagued demagogue-in-chief. It's about the past four years, not 400 years. Sheesh.

So, stop using the word "angry" whenever you are talking about any black politician, and especially Obama!

#2: Chicago

Ah, Chicago. The Windy City. Home of the Willis Tower (formerly Sears Tower), Wrigley Field, and the Magnificent Mile. Synonymous also with racism, especially when used in connection with Obama. Apparently when you use the word "Chicago", you are subtly calling attention to "the Chicago Way", which is meant as a disparaging remark because it means that the one embracing "the Chicago Way" is playing dirty, mean. And apparently only black people do that - play dirty, mean - and as such it's a code word for racist conservatives. As Chris Matthews elucidates:

"That sends that message: This guy's helping the poor people in the bad neighborhoods and screwing us in the 'burbs."

#3: Constitution (also: Founding Fathers)

That's right, apparently referring to the United States Constitution, that founding document that has never been equaled in all of human history either before or since, is really a racial code word. And if anyone should know, it would be Juan Williams of Fox News:

"The language of GOP racial politics is heavy on euphemisms that allow the speaker to deny any responsibility for the racial content of his message," Williams wrote. *"References to a lack of respect for the 'Founding Fathers' and the 'Constitution' also make certain ears perk up by demonizing anyone supposedly threatening core 'old-fashioned American values.'"*

This, of course, plays right in to the notion that the Tea Party, that group of people who want to return to the Constitution as the simple basis to run this country, is just a bunch of redneck racists. I wonder if they think the same about the Declaration of Independence too?

#4: Experienced (similar to: Qualified)

So, when Obama was first running for President back in 2008, there were plenty of people who were talking about his lack of experience. He had only been a Senator for barely over 300 in-session days when he announced his intention to run for President. This is just one of the reasons why people were claiming that he was inexperienced. Now, in his bid for re-election, folks are saying that his inexperience showed and has resulted in the state of national affairs today.

But wait a minute, they can't mean what they really mean. What they *REALLY* mean is that the word "experience" is actually a racial code word. Basil Smilke explains:

"Experienced? Does it really mean the time that he spent in the Senate, or does it mean, 'Well, does that guy have the same kind of experience in life that I have? Does he have an experience that I can relate to? Does he have the same kind of experience, uh, as a black person that I'm used to when I deal with black people.' What does inexperience really mean?"

Clearly, Basil, and others on the Left, have been hearing race for years when this word is used.

#5: Food Stamp President

This was made famous by former Republican Presidential candidate and Speaker of the House, Newt Gingrich. Almost as soon as he had finished uttering those words, Lefties were haranguing him as a racist. Interestingly, when one looks at the statistics for those who are on Food Stamps, it becomes painfully obvious that *white* people make up the majority of folks benefiting from this program. Newt, being as sharp and well-informed as ever, handed Chris his proverbial backside on his August 27, 2012 show *Hardball*:

"Why do you assume food stamp refers to blacks? What kind of racist thinking do you have? You're being a racist because you assume they're black!"

Chris Matthews tried desperately to dig his way out of this quandary, but only succeeded in making his hole deeper and wider. In the end, Chris had no answer for Newt's questions because *there is no racism!* Clearly Chris was reading into this what he wanted.

#6: Golf

Since when is mentioning a sport akin to racism? When it's used in connection with our nation's first black President, that's when. At the Republican National Convention, Senate Minority Leader Mitch McConnell was scheduled to give a speech on Wednesday evening. As often happens, an early release of the speech was sent out, and the folks at MSNBC got their hands on a copy. Upon reading through the speech, they immediately found something that they didn't like. Excerpt below:

"For four years, Barack Obama has been running from the nation's problems. He hasn't been working to earn reelection. He's been working to earn a spot on the PGA tour," McConnell is expected to say.

As most everyone knows, Obama has played more rounds of golf than any single President in history; it's his chosen sport to relax and enjoy. Republicans have used this as an illustration of how little focus the President is apparently putting on things like the economy. But for the Lefties at MSNBC, it's actually a racial code word. Martin Bashir and Lawrence O'Donnell explain:

"There are many, many, many rhetorical choices you can make at any point in any speech to make whatever point up want to make," MSNBC's Lawrence O'Donnell said. "If he wanted to make the point that you just suggested and I think he does want to make that point, they had a menu of a minimum of ten

different kinds of images that they could have raised. And I promise you, the speech writers went through rejecting three or four before they land order that one. That's the one they want for a very deliberate reason. That -- there's -- these people reach for every single possible racial double entendre they can find in every one of these speeches."

"I know these people are insensitive. I know these speech writers. I know the way they work. They do not have the same sensitivity level that other speech writers do. But when you get to the Tiger Woods reference, there were people in the speech writing room, I know this, without a shadow of a doubt, who said, 'Wait a minute, do we really want to go there? Do we really want to go to Tiger Woods and the vote and the room was yes, we do.' And Mitch McConnell agreed to do it," O'Donnell said.

"Wow. Things are getting lower and lower by the day," MSNBC's Martin Bashir said."

These people have race on the brain! What "racial double entendre" is Lawrence O'Donnell referring to in McConnell's speech? I've read through those few sentences a dozen times, trying to find where this is, and I can't find it. And since when is bringing up the name of Tiger Woods racist? He's a professional golfer, and he's damn good at it! That's racist?! Martin and Lawrence have a serious case of race-baiting, apparently seeing race everywhere, especially where there is none.

#7: Holding Down The Fort

Most of us have used this phrase from time to time. The common usage means that we want people to watch where ever they are at to make sure things stay safe and nothing of value is taken. Presumably this came from the days when forts were the military "safe houses" of the day, and those left in the fort had to keep it from being taken over by the enemy. Seems pretty straight forward, right? Nope, not according to the Chief Diversity Officer of the State Department, John Robinson. This is actually racially-coded language that is offensive. How? He explains in the department's July/August 2012 magazine issue:

"...but the phrase's historical connotation to some is negative and racially offensive. To "hold down the fort" originally meant to watch and protect against the vicious Native American intruders. In the territories of the West, Army soldiers or settlers saw the "fort" as their refuge from their perceived "enemy," the stereotypical "savage" Native American tribes."

He uses a ton of loaded language, denoted by the quotation marks around the key words: fort, enemy, and savage. I wonder if fort is some sort of coded language that might mean, oh, I don't know...*fort?!* Interesting how he qualifies the word "enemy" with the word "perceived". "Sorry, soldier, that man over there running at you with a knife or sword, intent on killing you, is only your *perceived* enemy. He's not really your enemy..." And why is it "the stereotypical 'savage' Native American tribes."? I've studied some history, and I would have to say that, by and large, most Native American tribes were anything but savage. The Chief Diversity Officer is completely all tied up in knots trying to make sure that people don't inadvertently use some racially-coded language, and it would be funny if it weren't so sad. To top it all off, before he launches into a litany of these racially-coded words, he says this:

"Much has been written about whether the etymologies below are true or merely folklore, but this isn't about their historical validity..."

Basically, he's stating that he has no idea if what he's talking about is true or not, but that doesn't matter! And why should it? He's only trying to make a point based on history, so who cares if the history that he's relating isn't actually true. When will this clown be fired?

#8: Kitchen Cabinet

Many of you, myself included, may not be familiar with this term. It was first coined back in the 1860s to describe then-President Andrew Jackson's unofficial team of advisers. The President obviously has an official Cabinet, but these folks are in addition to that official Cabinet and are often personal or family friends, business associates, and the like. Seems pretty straight forward, unless you are one who sees racism in nearly anything a conservative utters.

Case in point, radio talk-show host Mark Thompson. He had a major problem with Romney using this phrase at his NAACP speech in reference to his own personal, non-official confidant list, and the fact that he had a black person in his "kitchen cabinet" as governor and that he would continue to have this person in the same role as President. Apparently this is blatant racism on the part of Romney, but only because Mark Thompson and others didn't understand the historical reference. As I mentioned above, someone in a Presidential candidate's "kitchen cabinet" is a close associate, a confidant, a friend. Romney was saying that he had a black person as a close associate, a friend, and that he would keep him close when he became President.

What those who accuse Romney of racism *thought* he was saying was that he had a black person actually serving in his *kitchen!* Yes, they really thought that! Here's an example of what an attendee of his NAACP speech thought about Romney's "kitchen cabinet" statement:

"I cannot believe that guy is so inconsiderate to stand in front of a group of black people and talk about people being in his kitchen cabinet," she said. "Remember those were the good jobs for people during slavery, being in the big house, in the kitchen. We didn't find that very embracing. We don't want to be in your kitchen. And that's where we feel like all his jobs for us are going to be."

Talk-radio host Mark Thompson also didn't understand the reference:

"To talk about being in the kitchen and not talk about an African-American actually being in your cabinet is really not a good metaphor to use with African-Americans," he said disapprovingly.

I'll say it again: Romney was not talking about having a black person in the kitchen, but rather that he has, and will continue to have, a black person as a close, personal confidant. Learn your history people!

#9: Obamacare

Didn't know that was a racially-coded word, did you? You just thought it was a short-hand term that rightfully tied the Affordable Care Act to President Obama, who signed the bill into law. Silly racist! *The Daily Beast* writer Michael Tomasky says that Romney's use of the word was racist when he used it during his speech to the NAACP. Apparently, Romney only used the word in order to "get points from white moderates by appearing at the NAACP while generating high-fives on the white right...". Michael also claimed that Romney "wasn't a race-baiter until yesterday" (meaning the day he spoke to the NAACP). So, every other time that Romney had used the word "Obamacare" before the NAACP speech, he wasn't racist, but because he spoke to a predominantly black audience, that automatically makes the word racist. Wow, talk about your race-baiters, Michael Tomasky is it.

#10: Privileged

Rick Perry got into hot water during his Presidential run when he referred to Obama's upbringing as "privileged" and has "never had to go through what Americans [are now] going through." Normally, when one refers to someone else as "privileged", what that typically means is that they are in a more elite position to which most others do not belong. Having a Harvard degree typically is a privileged degree, as it carries with it prestige and honor that most degrees from other universities do not carry. Rick Perry was absolutely fine with using this word, but it was like throwing grease on a fire for the *Washington Post's* Jonathan Capehart. He explains:

"That's the dog whistle that Rick Perry is going for. The President was not raised privileged. He wasn't handed anything. He absolutely had to work for everything that he got. But for Rick Perry to say that President Obama was privileged and didn't have to work for what he got, the code is, he got into Columbia University, he got into Harvard University not through

merit, not because he's smart, but because he took the place of someone else through affirmative action, that someone else being someone white," Mr. Capehart said on Martin Bashir's MSNBC show.

Excuse me? Rick Perry never said that Obama didn't have to work for what he got, and he never said that Obama was raised privileged. Jonathan has to put words into Perry's mouth in order to setup the straw man: "he (Obama) got into Harvard...because he took the place of someone else through affirmative action, that someone else being someone white." Only Jonathan would hear this supposed "dog whistle" because he's a Lefty that sees almost everything through the racism lens. He completely missed the point that because of Obama's degree, which affords him a privileged status that most others don't enjoy, that he is insulated from things that have affected most folks of all colors.

#11: Professor

Apparently referring to Obama's stint as a professor at the University of Chicago also is off-limits due to it being a racially-coded word. Professor (oh, can I say that?) Charles Ogletree, in an interview with *Inside Higher Ed*, had this to say about the term:

Ogletree, founding and executive director of the Charles Hamilton Houston Institute for Race and Justice, says he sees the "professor" label as a thinly veiled attack on Obama's race. Calling Obama "the professor" walks dangerously close to labeling him "uppity," a term with racial overtones that has surfaced in the political arena before, Ogletree said."

I see, so we aren't actually referring to Obama in the correct sense when we refer to him as a professor, we're actually calling him "uppity". Professor Ogletree is a race-baiter himself since he apparently sees racism in almost any word or term.

And although Michelle Malkin had a great start, there are now other racially-coded words that we need to watch out for.

#12: Peanut Butter Sandwich

I can hear it now: You've got to be kidding me! Unfortunately, no, I'm not kidding, but I wish I were. Even the good old peanut butter sandwich is now a racially-charged word. How did this happen? Verenice Gutierrez, the principal at Harvey Scott K-8 School, explains:

Take the peanut butter sandwich, a seemingly innocent example a teacher used in a lesson last school year. "What about Somali or Hispanic students, who might not eat sandwiches?" says Gutierrez, principal at Harvey Scott K-8 School, a diverse school of 500 students in Northeast Portland's Cully neighborhood. "Another way would be to say: 'Americans eat peanut butter and jelly, do you have anything like that?' Let them tell you. Maybe they eat torta. Or pita."

Who really cares if a student eats a peanut butter sandwich or not? Who cares if they never eat a sandwich, of any kind, period? So because the Hispanic or Somali or any other student might not eat a sandwich, that makes the use of the sandwich as a food item for a lesson racist?! People like this principal see racism anywhere, and will scream it at the drop of a hat.

#13: Crime

It's now a racial crime to use the word 'crime'. Why? Well, according to the co-host of the MSNBC show The Cycle and Time Magazine columnist Touré, it's because...well...it's just become that way!

Like welfare, even though more whites commit crimes than blacks, the word is more associated with blacks who have historically been stereotyped as wild, violent, animalistic and immoral. As Michelle Alexander writes in The New Jim Crow, "What it means to be criminal in our collective consciousness has become conflated with what it means to be black, so the term white criminal is confounding, while the term black criminal is nearly redundant."

That's interesting, because I don't have a predetermined picture of what a criminal looks like. Why? Because criminals come in all varieties: male and female, tall and short, blond and black hair, etc. Touré even admits that more white people commit crimes in this country than blacks, but that apparently doesn't matter. Maybe he and Michelle Alexander live or grew up in a place that had a majority of crimes committed by black people, but that doesn't mean it was the same in the rest of the country. They are choosing to hear or see what they want, and they want to see racism everywhere, including criminals.

#14: Entitlement Society

Juan Williams, that liberal contributor at Fox News, who was too moderate for NPR and was fired, apparently also has his racial radar going at high speed. Back at the end of January of 2012, he wrote an article for *The Hill* magazine where he tore into racial code words used by the Republicans:

> *"The language of GOP racial politics is heavy on euphemisms that allow the speaker to deny any responsibility for the racial content of his message. The code words in this game are "entitlement society" — as used by Mitt Romney..."*

Apparently, Juan Williams must think that entitlements are a form of reparations, otherwise why would Romney and others use these words? There is nothing racial with the term "entitlement society", because that's the direction the country is really going. More and more people are receiving various handouts from the federal government, and they are coming to depend on them, and think that they are entitled to these handouts. Think about how Social Security works: money is taken from today's wage-earners and given to those that are retired; this is a wealth-transfer system. No, what's really going on here is that Lefties like Juan Williams don't want to talk about how the major entitlement areas of Social Security, Medicare and Medicaid are eating the lion's share of the federal budget every year, so they demonize those who aptly refer to our society in the way that Romney and many others do. They call them racists so that they can marginalize and silence them. Only race-baiters do that.

Part 2:
Just A Few Examples
Of Supposed Racism
(As Told By The Left)

Virginia State Senator
L. Louise Lucas

Date: July 24, 2012

Senator Louise Lucas is a state senator from Virginia. She also happens to be black and a member of President Obama's "Truth Team", and speaks on his behalf at different events around the state of Virginia. The Senator was appearing on a local radio station, AM1650, on the John Fredericks Show. The conversation had centered on politics, and at one point the senator moved the conversation in the direction of racism. Below is the exchange between the senator and the show host.

Fredericks: "Do you really believe now that this is still about race?"
Lucas: "I absolutely believe it's all about race, and for the first time in my life I've been able to convince my children, finally, that racism is alive and well."

Fredericks: "Even in Virginia?"
Lucas: "In Virginia? How about all across this nation - and *especially* in Virginia." (emphasis added)

It's all about race. She's not only convinced herself (long ago, it sounds like) but she's also convinced at least some of her family members of this as well. She sees racism everywhere, or at least everywhere in politics. If you think this way, you'll see racism in so many things, especially where there is no racism. Now think about this: Senator Lucas is a black person. From Virginia. Which, according to her, is *especially* full of racism.   Question: how did she then get elected? Answer: there is no racism, and she got elected fair and square.

What boggles the mind is that people like Senator Lucas really don't get that they are being completely ridiculous when they say things like this. So, Virginia is full of racists, yet they elected her, a black woman, multiple times, and they elected Barack Obama as President. I guarantee that if anyone pressed her on this point, she would simply make something up in order somehow show that racism is still rampant.

MSNBC & The Black
Racist With Guns

Date: August 18, 2009

On MSNBC's *Morning Meeting* program, host Contessa Brewer had a segment about President Obama holding a town hall meeting in Phoenix, Arizona, about the Affordable Care Act. In the segment, she focused on one man who had shown up at the event with a pistol on his belt and a semi-automatic rifle on a strap over his shoulder. He wasn't the only person there carrying a firearm; apparently nearly a dozen other individuals were also carrying firearms, but the segment focused on this one man and the fact that he had a semi-automatic rifle slung over his shoulder.

Contessa then brought in 2 other folks, Dylan Ratigan (who has since left MSNBC) and Touré, co-host of MSNBC's *The Cycle*, to start a discussion. There were a number of ways that she could have started things off, but this is how she chose to begin the 3-person discussion:

Brewer: "...and the reason we're talking about this, a lot of talk here, Dylan, because people feel like..yes, there are 2nd amendment rights, for sure, but also there are questions about whether this has racial overtones. I mean, here you have a man of color in the presidency and white people showing up with guns strapped to their waists or to their legs." (emphasis added)

Now, why would she immediately start off with "racial overtones" and referencing "white people"? For the record, Contessa Brewer is white, Dylan is white, and Touré is black. The answer is that they were trying to make race an issue with the President being black. They were making an assumption that all of the gun-carrying people were white, AND that they only showed up because the President is black. That MUST mean that the gun-carrying white people are racist. The conversation continued:

Touré: "It sounds simplistic when you put it that way, but it is real that there is tremendous anger in this country about government, the way government seems to be taking over the country, anger about a *black person being President*. Just several upheavals in the country over the last ten years from 9/11, to the economic tsunami, to the *black man becoming President* and, you know, we see these *hate groups* rising up and this is definitely part of that." (emphasis added)

Put together what he just said: 1) anger about government, 2) [anger] about the increase in the size and scope of government, and 3) anger about a black person being President. Who isn't happy about the size and scope of government? The Tea Party and other conservatives. Who isn't happy about a black person being President? Racists, white supremacists, KKK people, etc. And with what he said, Touré is linking the Tea Party and other conservatives with these racists, saying that they are all an angry group of people; that they are all one and the same people: racists.

Like I stated at the beginning of this book, Obama got an additional 30+ million votes from people who are not black. Is that racism? I hardly think so. Touré said at the end of his statement '...this is definitely part of that.', he was obviously referring to the man who had the handgun and AR-15 rifle and classifying that man as being a part of a hate group - you know, people that are angry about the size and scope of government, and people that are angry about having a black President. Now, nowhere else was it reported that the man in question was part of a hate group, nor was it ever reported that he was threatening anyone or causing any sort of commotion. Yet Touré knew that he was part of a hate group??

Two things about this story are important to point out, and expose the un-journalistic practices at MSNBC. The first is that the man in question with the handgun and AR-15 semi-automatic rifle is actually black. Yes, a black man was armed and attended the healthcare town hall. At no time during the discussion between these 3 people was it ever mentioned that the man they were using as an example of hate groups and racial tensions was himself a black person. The second is that the video they showed of this gun-carrying individual was edited in such a way that the color of his skin was never revealed. Even if the hosts/analysts didn't mention his color, the video could have, but alas it didn't.

Now, why would they do this? Why would dozens

of people who work on this show, both in front of and behind the cameras, do this? Answer: they have a race-baiting agenda. They were aiming to get people all worked up that white hate groups were showing up at events where the black President was in attendance. This just happened to be a nice double-whammy: racial tension and the 2nd amendment. This is blatant mis-reporting by these folks, and they should all be ashamed that they purposefully twisted the facts to try to manufacture a story from nothing. They were putting forth a racial narrative to make a story to get viewers. One can't get much lower than that.

MSNBC Host Ed Schultz
& Rick Perry

Date: August 15, 2011

MSNBC host Ed Schultz, on his show *The Ed Show* on August 15, 2011, did a segment about then-Republican Presidential candidate Rick Perry. Now, this would be just fine, as Rick Perry was in the race to become the Republican nominee for the 2012 Presidential campaign. Unfortunately, things started out on a sour note right from the get go, as you'll read here:

Schultz: "I think there's an element of racism *everytime* people claim the first black President doesn't love this country. Perry comes from the *radical* country club that loves to remind *white* Americans President Obama is 'other, not like you'. Perry also wants you to know that he's pro business." (emphasis added)

So this is how he introduces the clip of Rick Perry speaking on the stump in Iowa. Ed shows his cards right away with his first sentence where he thinks that 'everytime' someone claims Obama doesn't love this country it is due to them being racist. Here's my question: what if a black person was watching that particular episode of Ed's show and they had said that they felt that Obama didn't love America. Would that person be considered a racist? How could that be, if the President AND that person are both black? How does that work?

Ed continued by claiming that Rick came from a 'radical country club'. Exactly what is a radical country club? Where is it located? I'm guessing Ed knows, since he brought it up. Regardless of where this mythical country club is, the members are all about 'white Americans' - they want to tell these white Americans that President Obama is 'other, not like you'. What does this mean? It means that Rick Perry is a racist, according to illustrious Ed Schultz. And where is the evidence for this racism? Here is what Rick Perry said in the video that Ed played:

Perry: "I am a pro-business governor. I don't make any apologies about it and I will be a pro-business President. Getting America back to work is the most important issue that faces this country. Being able to pay off fourteen and a half or sixteen trillion dollars worth of debt. That big black cloud that hangs over America..."

The audio cuts out at this point, but the video continues on for another second or two. The screen then cuts back to Ed, who sums up everything with a single sentence:

Schultz: "That black cloud Perry is talking about is President Barack Obama."

Really? Is that what you thought he was talking about, Ed? Because that would be obviously racist if that's what he was talking about. And everybody would know about it, because ALL of the Republican Presidential candidates were getting copious amounts of television coverage on a daily basis, so surely there would be a huge outcry over these comments. How could Rick get away with such a racist statement? It has to be true, we just heard/read Rick's own words.

Only, that wasn't quite the truth. Remember just a couple of paragraphs above I mentioned that the audio cut out and the video kept playing for a second or so? Well, when you look at the full video, without the creative editing that was done by the show, it is as clear as water that Rick was *not* making a racist comment. The audio was purposefully cut to make it seem as if Ed was right in his analysis.

Facts are funny things, they have a way of coming out. The more outrageous the lie is from the facts, the faster the truth usually comes out. And plenty of other people knew what the facts were, and they called Ed and MSNBC on it. The very next day on his show, Ed played the full clip in context. Below is what Perry had really said:

Perry: "I am a pro-business governor. I don't make any apologies about it and I will be a pro-business President. Getting America back to work is the most important issue that faces this country. Being able to pay off fourteen and a half or sixteen trillion dollars worth of debt. That big black cloud that hangs over America, *that debt that is so monstrous. There's only one way you get rid of it that's practical, that makes sense. And* *that is to free up America. Free up American entrepreneurs."* (emphasis on additional footage aired)

Wow. I didn't hear or read anything racial at all in what Rick Perry said, did you? Yeah, I didn't think so. Rick was specifically talking about the national debt (which at the time of the writing of this book is nearing $16 trillion) and how it looms like a guillotine blade over a victim. Rick's proposed solution: to get more people to start businesses so that the U.S. economy can revive and grow and provide the increased tax revenues to help pay off the debt. And yet, because Ed Schultz and MSNBC had the agenda of making racism an issue in the Presidential campaign, they purposefully edited the video to make it look like Perry was saying something racist.

But that wasn't the worst part. At least they played the complete unedited video. Unfortunately, that's as far as things went for truth-telling on his show. When Ed was referring to his previous day's "error" he prefaced the clip in the following manner:

Schultz: "Now last night we played a clip of Governor Perry talking about the debt being a black cloud over this country. We did not present the full context of those statements, and we should have. Here's the full clip. Let's get it right, here's the full clip."

Notice that he doesn't even acknowledge the fact that just a day earlier he had accused Rick Perry of racism. He also tries to pretend that he didn't use a racial angle on the previous day's playing of the edited clip. Instead, he insisted that they played the clip because Perry was talking about the debt. Really? Because I just went back and looked at the transcript above and that's not the reason you played the clip in the first place. So, they play the full, unedited clip, and then Ed has one more opportunity to come clean:

Schultz: "No doubt about it, it was a mistake and we regret the error. On this particular statement we should not have included it in our coverage of his overheated rhetoric. That's our mistake."

Overheated rhetoric? What the hell is Ed talking about? This is simply his way of brushing the previous day's race-baiting segment under the rug, making it seem that the previous day's racial fabrication never happened. What a tool.

Aurora, Colorado Shootings...
About Race?

Date: July 23, 2012

MSNBC talking head Touré, apparently so sophisticated that he only needs a first name, co-hosts the show *The Cycle* and also appears as a guest on other shows. During this particular show installment, he felt he had to inject race into the horrible Aurora, Colorado shooting disaster. Here is a transcript of his comments:

Touré: "We never have this debate until we have a tragedy and then its over emotionalized, its over fraught [sic], you can't have a substantive debate when everybody's so sensitive.

"Day to day crime, as we've talked about, has fallen over the last 20 years so I think the average voter feels less of the fear that would motivate lawmakers to do something. These spectacular mass killings are way up from when our dads were kids -- I think there was something like 11 in the 50s and 60s and over 550 in the last part of the last century a decade ago.

"So, those things sort of make us think about these things, but we understand those are outlier crimes, somebody going to shoot up the mall or shoot up the school. I would hope that it would be something like a Trayvon Martin situation that would make people think, 'Wow. wrongful death, even though it's a legal gun owner. How do we move forward from this situation?' But so much of this issue, I think comes down to, 'Let's make sure law abiding *white people* are able to have access to guns and make sure that *black criminals* are not and that becomes part of the locus of the problem.

"And we don't even want to talk about that sort of *racial, black sort of bottom of it all*, but that's definitely part of it." (emphasis added)

We'll ignore the first couple of paragraphs; that's another discussion for another day. It's only when he gets to the third paragraph that his true feelings/intentions come out. First, why is he bringing in the Trayvon Martin case? What does that have to do with the Aurora, Colorado shooting? Answer: they have nothing to do with each other, unless you, like Touré, believe that the Trayvon Martin case is actually a case of a white man shooting and killing a defenseless black man/kid. Then, he makes a stark statement in that he believes that the whole narrative is to arm 'white people' and to disarm or prevent arming 'black criminals'. Really? He's going to claim that racism is the root of these shootings (both Aurora and Trayvon)?

It sounds like he's saying that 'white people' owning guns is a bad deal. Is it? No, it is not. Is it bad for 'black people' to own guns? Again, no it is not. But notice he doesn't say 'black people', he says 'black *criminals'*. Is it bad for criminals, of any color, to own guns? I think we would all agree that yes, it is bad for criminals, of any color, to own guns.

So why is this young man, Touré, so keen on turning this into a racial case? Because that's probably what he's grown up with and been indoctrinated with. He doesn't want to look at all of the evidence, because if he did he would find out that racism is not as rampant as he would have you believe. But he's built for himself a really nice niche in the news world at MSNBC, where he, being black, can offer the appropriate black perspective on the events of the day. He's the one that can put things in their proper perspective. Give me a break.

Chris Matthews
& "The Grand Wizard Crowd"

Date: April 23, 2012

Chris Matthews, host of the MSNBC show *Hardball* as well as the Sunday political show *The Chris Matthews Show*, had on 2 guests to discuss Romney and some of his recent comments while on the stump. The guests were former RNC chairman Michael Steele and *The Huffington Post* editorial director Howard Fineman. Now, the conversation was going along just fine, with discussions starting out around how the Democrats and President Obama should be going after Mitt Romney in the campaign. All well and good, certainly expected, and no different from what is going on all over cable news. But then things take an interesting turn when Chris starts to paint Romney as an out of touch person by using phrases like "flat-earther" and someone who doesn't believe in evolution. Then things take a sad turn when host Chris Matthews says a very revealing thing: he refers to those in the Republican party as "the Grand

Wizard Crowd". Fortunately, Michael Steele is a good enough man to call Matthews on it right then and there, and Chris backtracks from his comments, but not without getting in a jab about 'birthers'.

Now, there's actually a number of things that I noticed when researching this particular story. First, in watching the video of the exchange between Steele and Matthews, it really seems to me that Chris is only putting on an *act* of being remorseful. I don't believe that he really is. Maybe he was just embarrassed to have been caught saying such a thing, and on camera no less, but I have a hunch that he actually got caught up in the discussion and was a little annoyed that Michael Steele was calling his bluff when he (Matthews) tried to paint Romney as a right-wing loon (my words, not Chris's). I really believe that Chris let it slip that he thinks most if not all of the Republican party are a bunch of racists, apparently including the *BLACK* former RNC chairman Michael Steele.

The second thing that I found is with the transcript from that day's show. I went directly to the source, *Hardball*'s section on the MSNBC website. And I listened and watched the video while double-checking the transcript, and do you know what I found? They didn't transcribe it accurately! If you listen to the video and follow along with the transcript, what you'll find is that Chris's "Grand Wizard Crowd" statement is lacking a few key words. I wrote out what I heard from the video and then listed out what is from the transcript below.

(video) Matthews: "Okay, let's go [mumbling] well it certainly was...well you're...the Grand Wizard crowd over there. Anyway, look, look..."

(transcript) Matthews: "Okay, it certainly was on the grand wizard over there. Anyway, look..."

Can you see the difference? And when Michael calls him on it, he (Michael) asks Matthews if he (Matthews) thinks that the Republican party are the Ku Klux Klan. Like the "Grand Wizard Crowd" comment, the "Ku Klux Klan" reference has also been scrubbed from the transcript.

(video) Steele: "Are you saying that we're the Ku Klux Klan? Give me a break. We didn't... Don't, don't go there with me on that."

(transcript) Steele: "Give me a break. Don't go there with me on that, all right?"

The portion of Steele talking and asking the "Ku Klux Klan" question was labeled "(CROSSTALK)" in the transcript immediately preceeding Steele's words. Now why would MSNBC take these words out? I think it's obvious that they don't want to have one of their primary political hosts shown as a possible racist and making references to Grand Wizards and the KKK. This is all just a bunch of race-baiting that backfired on Chris Matthews.

Believe it or not, that isn't all that I found. When looking at the comments section of *The Huffington Post*, whose article I linked to for some of this research, I found a host of negative comments, some of which were racial in nature. And below is one of Chris Matthews's fans, I'm sure:

Commenter: "Matthews is exactly correct and Michael Steele is an Oreo."

So, first we have this commenter believing that Chris Matthews is right, that the Republican party is basically a bunch of KKK members, Grand Wizards if you will, and the only thing that they stand for is white supremacy. But the commenter goes on to show their true nature by calling Michael Steele an "Oreo".

Now, what does it mean to call someone an "Oreo"? Well, think about it. A traditional Oreo cookie as 3 parts: a white center and black/dark halves holding the center in. What the commenter is really saying is that, on the inside, Michael Steele is really a white person. His skin color might be black, but he's been taken in by the white people, so much so that he acts white even though he looks black. It's meant to be a disparaging remark, and I think it definitely is.

All of these people, the commenter and those like him/her, as well as Chris Matthews are trying to continue to foment racial strife. Sometimes, like those of the commenter perhaps, it is because they really do think racism is a huge problem, and sometimes, like Chris Matthews I'm suspecting, is so that they can make a story out of nothing.

Christian Science Monitor
& Racism

Date: July 23, 2012

The Christian Science Monitor is a weekly news magazine that was started by the founder of The First Church of Christ, Scientist: Mary Baker Eddy. She started the magazine in 1908 when she was 86 years old. According to their website, *The Christian Science Monitor* is a news magazine first and foremost, with the goal of bringing news (according to their mission statement) "to injure no man, but to bless all mankind". A very lofty goal, and one that they have maintained for over 100 years.

However, not all was as it seemed in a Commentary piece written for a later July edition. The title of the piece was "Is a pro-Romney ad racist? Five questions to ask yourself". It was written by NYU professors Charlton McIlwain and Stephen Caliendo. Here is the first paragraph of the article.

In the Presidential election, it's not a matter of whether racism will appear in campaign messaging, but when. President Obama is running for reelection with the support of the majority of black and Latino voters. Mitt Romney is challenging Mr. Obama with an almost exclusively white constituency behind him. Both candidates will raise and spend unprecedented amounts of money on political advertisements, as will their respective parties and allied super PACs.

It's plainly obvious that these 2 professors are convinced that racism is alive and well in the United States. I mean, read the first sentence! It's not a matter of whether, it's a matter of when? Well, surely they must mean that it could come from either side of the political aisle, right? Well, no, that's not right. If it were, then they wouldn't have written the above paragraph in the way they did. It is easy to see that they are already convinced that Romney will be putting out racist ads, and they want to provide you a way to tell when they are aired.

But let's have the professors explain to us these 5 questions and how they are to be used. Here are the 5 questions, and we'll go through them individually in more detail.

1. Does the ad reference racial stereotypes?
2. Does the ad show Obama's image alongside a racial stereotype?
3. Are all the people surrounding Romney white?
4. Does the ad create an 'us' versus 'them' racial contrast?
5. Is the audience where the ad runs mostly white?

Before we get into the questions, I want to point out

that, until now, no one had ever (to my knowledge) attempted to point out where a particular campaign's advertisements were racist. So why would they now? Because we have the first black President in our nation's history, and in order to keep him there, and by association make it easier for other black people to ascend to this highest position, folks like these professors need to make people feel guilty, need to make them feel and think that they might be racist, and by doing so they will make those people vote to keep Obama in the White House to prove that they aren't racist. But, let's dissect the questions to make sure that what I'm suggesting is correct.

1. Does the ad reference racial stereotypes?

This first question seems pretty straight forward, but my question is this: what is an example of a racial stereotype? They don't answer that question, probably because they don't want to paint themselves into a corner. But the authors did feel the need to expand further on this question by adding additional questions to help direct you on how to properly determine if the ad really does reference racial stereotypes. The first question they add is this:

Does the ad reference a long-standing racial stereotype historically associated with African-Americans?

I have no idea what that means. What is a "long-standing racial stereotype historically associated with African-Americans"? Unfortunately, the authors don't give us any examples, so one could very well assume, which I do, that they don't have any ideas either. But the next question is even worse:

Does it (the ad) state or suggest that President Obama is untrustworthy or prone toward criminality?

Seriously! I can tell you with certainty that EVERY Presidential campaign has had ads where one party attempted to portray the other party as untrustworthy. It always happens, whether it is true or not. But now, just because the President is black, that AUTOMATICALLY makes the ad a racist ad. Even in the off chance that what is being stated in the ad is true, it doesn't matter because the ad is, first and foremost, racist due to the allegations of untrustworthiness. I would also like to ask the authors of the article exactly where the "untrustworthiness" stereotype came from for blacks. I haven't seen that stereotype portrayed in my own life and environment.

The authors provide a link to a Romney ad on YouTube that they claim is a racist ad. The authors support this claim because the ad "has the effect of presenting the untrustworthiness stereotype...". Again, just because the President is black, that means its racist. I wonder what they would say if President Obama ran a similar ad against Mitt Romney. Would that be racist? Of course not, because Romney is white.

2. Does the ad show Obama's image alongside a racial stereotype?

Here again the authors point to the same ad used for the first question. Because the ad connects the concept of "lying" with Obama, that is a racial stereotype and as such means the ad is racist. Because of course black people in general are just known liars and white folks are as truthful as the day is long. Pardon me while I vomit. Have the authors never encountered a white person who was a liar? I have, many times. So again, even if the ad were true and Obama did lie, because that's a racial stereotype it means that the ad, and by association, Romney is a racist.

3. Are all the people surrounding Romney white?

This is just a ridiculous question on its face! Because a particular ad might not have any black people in it, that automatically means the ad is racist? I didn't realize that we had a quota system for campaign ads now. Should we be making a list to ensure that the ads contain the proper amount of minorities? Got the black person? Check! Got the hispanic person? Check! Got the Native American person? Whoops, get that one in the picture, pronto! It's absurd to make that sort of leap where because you don't see any black people in the ad, that means that the ad and the candidate are racist. Perhaps at the rally, where the video clip was shot, there were black people, but they just weren't in the vicinity of the camera. Is that possible? Or maybe Romney visited an area where there are few or no black people living. If they don't live there, how would you expect to see them? Perhaps the camera operator was black, but because he/she isn't in the picture one assumes that there were no black people. Couldn't that also be a possibility? Of course all of these are possible, but the authors didn't think of that, instead immediately concluding that because they didn't see any black people, that means it's a racist ad. Pathetic.

4. Does the ad create an 'us' versus 'them' racial contrast?

Now this question requires a little bit more thought and discernment because you need to read between the lines. Because an ad by the Romney campaign may not have a black person in it (hey, remember that quota system from question #3!), when he uses the phrases "we" or "us", he's obviously referring to "white people" and therefore it's a racist ad. Here's my question: if Obama did the same thing, having only black people in an ad, and used words like "we" or "us", could that be considered racist as well? I mean, he would only be referring to "black people" and not also including white people, right? The authors are doing the same "divide-and-conquer" bit that others have done, because it's easier to control smaller groups. They are also causing you, the reader, to think about what you are viewing and if perhaps he really is a racist. This is pure nonsense, of course, because again the authors don't know (or if they do they are conveniently leaving that information out) if there might be black people off camera, or if the camera operator is black, or if the area where the gathering occurred doesn't have any black people living there, etc. They make a lot of assumptions in order to come to the conclusion that it's a racist ad.

5. Is the audience where the ad runs mostly white?

If the third question was ridiculous, this one is downright insulting. Basically what they mean is, if Romney runs an ad against Obama anywhere that there are "mostly white" people living, the ad is racist. Seriously, that's what they mean! The only proof of racism now is just where the ad plays. The authors are now reaching so far it's pathetic, and they've lost all credibility with this question. By that logic, a car commercial that features a white person that is aired in an area where "mostly black" people are living, that ad is racist. I'll guarantee, if you ask the authors that, they will backpeddle so fast it will make your head spin.

This entire commentary is a huge race-baiting scheme by the two professors. It's a completely one-sided argument that only applies to the Romney campaign and their ads, but they will give a complete pass on similar ads done by the Obama campaign. And yet, as insane as this article is, they will probably remain in their positions at NYU without so much as a peep from the university. Shameful, simple shameful.

Drudge Report = Racist

Date: June 15, 2012

Bill Maher, that wonderful comedian who hosts a show on HBO called *Real Time with Bill Maher*, did a segment on racism and Matt Drudge. On the June 15th show, Bill attempted to prove that the Right is just chock full of racists. How did he do this? By showing a number of photos of black people under the "Drudge Report" logo. These photos had appeared on the Drudge Report's website at various times during the month of April. The people that he showed, in order, are:

Mike Tyson
Louis Farrakhan
Marion Barry
Rev. Jeremiah Wright
Al Sharpton and Eric Holder
Michael Jordan

Now, why exactly does the Drudge Report showing pictures of black people when they are tied to a specific article - which, by the way, was written by someone other than Matt Drudge - why is this deemed to be racist? Drudge has pictures of different people up on his website all the time in connection with various articles that he aggregates. Since he shows pictures of women who are in the news, such as Michelle Obama and Hillary Clinton, does that mean Matt Drudge is a sexist? Of course not! And yet, people like Bill Maher feel the need to scream racism at the drop of a hat.

What's also interesting is that Bill had his staff go through not a current month, like the month of June when the segment aired, but they went back to the month of April. Why April? Okay, I'll give him the benefit of the doubt and suggest that when the program was taped it really was April or the first part of May, so April would have been a fine time to do it. By why do it at all? If that's all it takes to show racism is to throw up a bunch of pictures and associate it with someone, then we're all in for some big problems. Bill Maher, whom I'll gladly call a race-baiter, should have his show canceled, but I somehow doubt that will happen.

So now, since Bill Maher showed pictures of black people on his show, does that mean he's a racist too? Just asking…

Representative Maxine Waters & God

Date: May 20, 2012

California Democratic Representative Maxine Waters likes to attend church. Good for her! She also likes to talk a lot. Again, that's good, we have freedom of speech. Unfortunately, it's what she chooses to say that isn't so good. And on top of that she says this in church. Ouch!

What did Representative Maxine Waters say that was so bad? Well, like many good Democrats, she says things in a way that, unless you are listening with a discerning ear, you might miss. Word choice incredibly important, as she illustrates with what she says toward the end of the video I transcripted.

Rep. Waters: "And so, pastor when those people are messing with me in Washington, D.C., and they come after me 'cause I'm trying to help poor people, and *people of color*, I said they ain't seen nothin' yet. 'Cause I don't know how to stop fighting." (emphasis added)

So first, we need to know who the 'they' are that she refers to. 'They' are the Tea Party, which she had referenced earlier in the video clip. Second, she uses the phrase 'people of color', which is obviously code words for 'blacks'. I find it interesting that she separates poor people and 'people of color' (blacks); that must mean that poor people are not necessarily black, otherwise why separate them? And if not all blacks are poor, why are you fighting for them, trying to help them? Oh, yes! That's because of the wide-spread racism that's still rampant in this country. And especially the Tea Party!

So, if she's accusing the Tea Party of coming after her because she's helping 'people of color' (blacks), that must mean that the Tea Party is racist, because if they weren't then they would want to help 'people of color' (blacks) just as much as she does. This is veiled language that she and many others on the Left are guilty of using, along with attempting to segregate out 'people of color' (blacks). Only when you are trying to divide and conquer do you separate people in different groups so that you can more easily deal with them. Shameful language by a race-baiting Representative.

The Un-Fair Campaign

Date: October, 2011

In the northern Minnesota city of Duluth, racism is lurking. Racism not just in tiny little pockets. No, this is racism on a city-wide basis. It's so prevalent, so ingrained in people and they just don't realize it. Because they don't realize it, the University of Minnesota - Duluth is sponsoring and supporting, along with other supporting partners, a new outreach program titled the "Un-Fair Campaign".

What is this campaign all about? Essentially, the group claims that "the system" (they don't explain what that is) was and is set up only for white people. Because of this exclusivity, racism is being practiced but most folks don't realize it. As such, "the system" is "un-fair" to everyone except white people, and in order to change that this group needs to inform people that they need to think about everything that they do to make sure that they aren't inadvertently reinforcing "the system" that was set up for white people; they need to try to make everything inclusive for all people.

Now, this sounds good, until you dig deeper into things. First, there's the problem with a video they have out featuring white people who are confessing their guilt for being white. What?! Why should they be guilty for being white? Was it a choice they made when they were born? *"Uh, yeah, what color skin would you like to have, little Johnny? White? Okay, there you go!"* Is the group saying that these white people are guilty because of "the system"? First off, what is "the system" that is being talked about, and did any of them actually mastermind "the system" to be for whites only? Hardly! Basically, the video is meant for whites to feel ashamed for being white, as if they were guilty already but didn't realize it. Funny, I thought in this country we were innocent until proven guilty.

So, the city of Duluth has racism running rampant through the population, but it's of a nature that folks just don't even realize that they are, in fact, racists. They are, according to this campaign, beneficiaries of 'white privilege'. What is 'white privilege'? Here's a list of examples of what constitutes 'white privilege':

* I can walk around a department store without being followed
* I can come to a meeting late and not have my lateness attributed to my race
* I am able to drive my car in any neighborhood without being perceived as being in the wrong place or looking for trouble
* I can turn on the television or look to the front page and see people of my ethnic and racial background represented
* I can take a job without my co-workers suspecting that I got it because of my racial background
* I can send my 16-year-old out with his new driver's

license and not have to give him a lesson in how to respond if police stop him

These are pretty ridiculous when you stop to think about them. Taking a job without your co-workers thinking you got it because of your racial background? Newsflash: You can't prevent people from thinking whatever they want! Did you get the job because of your racial background? If you didn't, then why do you care what others think? If you did, are you qualified? If not, perhaps you shouldn't have relied on Affirmative Action or another moronic government intrusion to get a job. If you're smart, hard working, dependable, timely and motivated, you'll get the job without a problem.

Do you really turn on the TV and not see people of a variety of different backgrounds? I do, all of the time. Maybe you need to branch out and turn the channel every once in a while, hmmm? And coming in late to a meeting...due to your RACE? Seriously, if you came late to a meeting, I don't care about your race, I care that you just have no sense of time-management and have wasted your own time and that of everyone else in the meeting.

Sending out your teenager with their NEW drivers license and you DON'T sit them down and talk about what to do if you are stopped by the police? I think that's pretty poor parenting, not giving your child the benefit of your knowledge and experience in matters dealing with vehicles, traffic, etc. That's not a sign of racism if you do that, that's a sign of a caring, compassionate parent who wants their child to have the benefit of their knowledge.

All of this is intended to foster white guilt, as if that is the antidote for all of this supposed racism. White people have all of the power, and they need to give it up so that others have a chance like they do, or so the thinking of the "Un-Fair Campaign" goes. This is just sinister race-baiting because it involves playing on people's guilt for something that they have never done.

Oppose 'You Didn't Build That'? Racist!

Date: July 27, 2012

I'm sure most of us have heard the "speech heard 'round the world" given by President Obama in early July. Probably the most famous line from that speech is 'you didn't build that'. Romney pounced on the comment, Obama backpeddled from it, and Obama supporters worked to try to diffuse the issue. One of the ways in which Obama supporters tried to diffuse the issue was saying that Romney had taken the President's comments out of context. This is a laughable joke, because when you actually put his comments in context, they sound *worse*, not better. So this line fizzled fairly quickly. So what is their next line of attack? Racism!

New York Magazine published a seemingly innocent-sounding article titled "The Real Reason 'You Didn't Build That' Works". The author, Jonathan Chait, was going to explain why Romney's ads worked well with the Republican/conservative crowd. It's unfortunate that he starts out the piece by lying.

Chait: "Mitt Romney's plan of blatantly lying about President Obama's 'you didn't build that' speech is clearly drawing blood. But what makes the attack work so well is not so much the lie itself but the broader subtext of it. Watch Obama's delivery in the snippet put together by this Republican ad:"

Romney didn't lie about Obama's speech; everyone has heard the speech in total. Nothing was taken out of context, he simply used the most damning piece of video from the speech. And he has no need to apologize for that. But that's not the worst part. What Jonathan is really after is "the subtext of it". That's why he calls for readers to view the ad in question, and specifically to watch Obama's delivery of his own words.

Chait: "The key thing is that Obama is angry, and he's talking not in his normal voice but in a "*black dialect*". This strikes at the core of Obama's entire political identity: a soft-spoken, reasonable African-American with a Kansas accent. From the moment he stepped onto the national stage, Obama's deepest political fear was being seen as a "traditional" black politician, one who was demanding redistribution from white America on behalf of his fellow African-Americans." (emphasis added)

Black dialect? I've watched this ad in particular a number of times, and the speech in total, and I NEVER thought he was angry or talking in a "black dialect". What I saw was passion in how he delivered the speech, conviction of his words. This is what people would want in the politician that they choose to support; they don't want wimps in office. Essentially what Jonathan is saying here is that Romney is a racist because of the particular video clip that is used in the ad. What I find interesting here is that in actuality, *Jonathan* is the one I suspect of being racist. Why would he say that viewers need to "watch Obama's delivery" in the ad, and then after the video say that Obama was speaking in a "black dialect". I didn't know what a black dialect was, and I still don't, because like I stated above he was speaking with passion.

This again is race-baiting by a magazine reporter, and by association the magazine as a whole, that is trying desperately to keep Obama looking shiny and electable while disparaging his opponent with lies and distortion. It's also unfortunate that there will be folks who will agree with him and will buy into the supposed racism that Jonathan had to make up.

Racist Romney...At The NAACP?

Date: July 11, 2012

Mitt Romney gave a speech at the NAACP where several times throughout his speech he was booed by members of the audience. According to the ABC News report on the event, Romney was booed when he said he'd repeal the healthcare law, when he said Obama's record proves that he (Obama) hasn't done enough on the economy and other matters, and when he said that he (Romney) would be a President who makes the lives of African-Americans better. Interestingly, there were some people who came out and said that Romney had planned all along to get booed at the gathering. One of those people was Touré, one of the co-hosts of *The Cycle* on MSNBC.

Touré: "Why would he bother going to the NAACP convention to get booed? Because the real audience wasn't in the room. He wanted to be booed by that black audience so that *white conservatives* — who still don't see him as one of them — and *white undecideds* would see that he's unafraid to *talk down* to black people, to offend them, to be their villain, to make them boo. The result is that he comes off looking tough or gains sympathy. Either way, he gets a soundbite that will bounce through the cable news echo chamber and elicit an emotional reaction from white voters. Romney's performance wasn't intended to win more black votes, it was intended to help win more white votes."

This guy Touré is just a flame-thrower of racism! He really thinks that "white conservatives" and "white undecideds" view themselves as superior, hence his word choice of Romney being "unafraid to talk down" to black people. Give me a friggin break! Romney went through the same litany of items that he usually goes through in his speeches, but somehow when he gives it in front of the NAACP he's talking to the "white people" out there so that they'll see how tough he is. And why, Touré, do "white conservatives" and "white undecideds" not see Romney as "one of them"? I don't know, because you never explained it; its as if everyone already knew that, just like you knew that Romney was only playing to his white base of supporters.

What a race-baiting low life Touré is! He doesn't just see things as black and white, but more like black VERSUS white, and that's just a sad way to live your life. You don't think that Romney could appeal to some folks at the NAACP who agree with his policy stances? And just for the record, Romney received a standing ovation at the end of his speech to the NAACP. Not too bad for a supposed racist white guy.

Now A Banner Is Racist?!

Date: April 19, 2012

Republican Presidential candidate Mitt Romney went to Ohio in mid-April. He gave a speech - not unusual for a Presidential candidate to do - but for some, it wasn't the speech they were paying attention to. Instead, it was the large banner behind him that they were focused on. What was it about the banner that caused them to stare, and then become outraged?

It's because the banner was black with white lettering. And that it read "Obama Isn't Working". Yes, really, that's why they are upset. Specifically, Tommy Christopher at MediaIte.com is convinced that "The slogan is a multiple entendre...", and on top of that the color choice was racist as well. Tommy explains:

Tommy: "When I first saw the banner this afternoon, the multiple meanings were clear: President Obama's policies aren't working, the Obama presidency isn't working, President Obama...isn't working, as in, doing any work. That's not a nice thing to say about any President, but like it or not, it becomes a more loaded accusation when leveled at our first black President."

Yup, that's exactly what I thought of when I saw the slogan, that Obama isn't doing any work (end sarcasm). Putting all of his golf outings aside, I'm sure that Obama does work; there are too many things that involve the presidency and he is required to address them on a daily basis. No, what I saw in that banner was this: the Obama policies aren't working, Obama's vision for America isn't working. Even Tommy himself said essentially the same thing when he started his comments. I definitely didn't think that it was Obama himself that isn't (physically) working. That would be a really low blow for anyone to level at *ANY* President, not just Obama. Yet, Tommy thinks that not only does the banner mean that Obama doesn't do any physical work, but that it's also a subtle racist jab because Obama is black, and so is the banner.

But why the black color as the background of the banner? Simple: the white lettering stands out better and can be read from further away. It's basic contrasting colors, people! If you put a light color against a dark color, you can see it (whatever "it" is: lettering, a design, etc.) from further away. Here's another thing to keep in mind about the banner: the colors mirror the colors used on Romney's specialty website ObamaIsntWorking.com. And really, it's not black that is on the banner background, it's a charcoal gray. Get a grip race-baiters!

You Lie, Boy!

Date: September 9, 2009

Early in his term, President Obama liked to use the national stage to try to make his case, especially when it came to the Affordable Care Act. In early September, 2009, the President held a televised speech and one of the main topics of his speech was that pending legislation. For weeks and months before this speech, and during the speech, President Obama had made many claims about the legislation and what it would do for America.

Now, many people, myself included, had started to tear apart the bill and learn what was in it. And what was in it wasn't good. In fact, many of the things that the President and others were claiming either would or wouldn't happen, in fact would be just the opposite. And this had been building for a while. Finally, during a nationally televised Presidential address, Representative Joe Wilson couldn't take the lies any longer and yelled out "liar" loud enough to be picked up by microphones.

This outburst encapsulated what many had been feeling for months, yet it was still disrespectful of the office of the President.

However, that's not *quite* how Maureen Dowd, columnist for the New York Times, heard it. From how she tells it, what she heard was "You lie, boy!". What does she mean with this? Simply that Representative Joe Wilson is a racist. She claims "Wilson clearly did not like being lectured and even rebuked by the *brainy black President* presiding over the majestic chamber.". (emphasis added) And now the President is "a black man whose legitimacy is constantly challenged by a loco fringe."

No, Maureen got it wrong; she had no idea what Joe Wilson was really objecting to. What Joe Wilson didn't like was the lies continuing to be perpetuated by the leader of the free world. And according to Maureen Dowd, people like Representative Wilson are a "loco fringe" questioning Obama's legitimacy. Funny, I've never heard that about the Representative, and most everyone else you ask will agree that Obama was elected fair and square. No, this is another Leftist that is trying to redirect the conversation by calling racism when there was none so that we won't focus on the horrible job President Obama has done.

Romney Campaign Ad Racist...
Yet True!

Date: August 8, 2012

The Romney Presidential campaign had put out an ad talking about how the Obama administration is "gutting" the 1996 Welfare Reform Act. How, exactly, is the administration doing this? The Heritage Foundation has done a great service in breaking down exactly how this is done, but essentially Health & Human Services secretary Kathleen Sebelius is reading authority into the bill that was never there. She is then consequently using this new-found authority to expand the definition of "work" to be much more than it was originally meant when the bill was passed and signed into law.

But, this isn't the problem. The REAL problem is that Romney is using code words and images in such a way that he's a racist. Or at least, so says Cheryl Contee of JackAndJillPolitics.com. Cheryl goes through a very messy, convoluted explanation that attempts to prove that Romney is a racist, but since he can't do it overtly, he needs to be very subtle and put things between the lines, which of course only other racists would see. Oh, and Cheryl, of course, because she's been looking hard to break this all down for us.

So, how is Romney racist with this ad? Okay kids, follow along and don't get lost! First, she explains that the ad really isn't about welfare, because Congress had recently (February, 2012) passed an extension of unemployment benefits. So, because both political parties "claimed victory", as she put it, then the ad can't possibly be about welfare. Just impossible!

Well, then, what is the ad really about? This is where Cheryl just flies off of the planet and goes into her own little universe. A universe where racism by whites is everywhere, coded into the very campaign ads we see. First, she refers to a USA Today article from March of 2012 where, in three states, the Public Policy Polling of Raleigh, NC, indicates that a significant number of GOP primary voters think that President Obama wasn't born in the United States.

Hmmm, let me think about that a moment. So, is Cheryl implying that those folks in those three states that think that President Obama wasn't born in the United States...are racists?! In a word: yes. How does she come to that conclusion? It's because Romney picked "a racially-coded ad that implies that Obama is somehow to the left of...Bill Clinton.". How did he do this? By showing only one black face - President Obama's. This, in Cheryl's expert opinion, is the nugget, the central piece, as she explains:

Cheryl: "The spot's coded message is designed to appeal to those that still believe Obama is a *Kenyan socialist muslim* whose primary purpose in the White House is to take the hard-earned tax dollars of all the working class *whites* working so hard in Romney's welfare ad and give it to every *lazy, shiftless nigger* in the United States who wants to sit at home, smoke dope and watch Maury all day long." (emphasis added)

Unbelievable! It's unfathomable that someone would go to such lengths to attempt to prove that a campaign ad is racist. She makes some incredible leaps and assumptions in her thinking that defy all logic. Basically, she is also stating that these racist folks, to whom the ad is meant to appeal, think that the only reason that Obama is in the White House is to obtain reparations of sorts for "every lazy, shiftless nigger" in the country. Really? She got all of that from a simple 30-second ad about an over-reaching secretary in his administration?

This is nothing more than race-baiting by Cheryl and her ilk. She's reading something into an ad where nothing of the sort exists. Why? Because she needs to keep Obama in office, no matter how bad of a job he's done as President. She's got an ax to grind, and yet she's become successful in speaking her mind on the Internet IN SPITE OF all of the racism that's apparently rampant in this country. What a sad person she is.

Romney Engaging
In 'Niggerization'?!

Date: August 16, 2012

Touré was at it again on the MSNBC show *The Cycle*. One of the co-hosts, Krystal Ball, started out the segment by introducing a set of video clips where she indicated that Mitt Romney was out with "a new attack line". My transcription of the video clips, which come from August 14, 2012, follow:

Romney: "His campaign and his surrogates have made wild and reckless accusations that disgrace the office of the presidency... This is what an angry and desperate presidency look like... Mr. President, take your campaign of division and anger and hate back to Chicago..."

Krystal then comes back and indicates that to her, the words Romney used "seem kind of loaded". She never explains what she means by that, but instead defers to Touré, who has no problem explaining what he thought was going on.

Touré: "Yeah, I mean, that really bothered me. You notice he says 'anger' twice. He's really trying to, um, use the racial coding, and access some really deep stereotypes about the 'angry black man'. Um, this is part of the playbook against Obama, the 'otherization', he's not like us. I know it's a heavy thing, I don't say it lightly, but this is 'niggerization', you are not one of us, and that you are like the 'scarey black man' who we've been trained to fear and, the idea of, of locating anger around Barack Obama just doesn't fit with who he is and who he's trained himself to be going back to high school, training himself to be 'no drama Obama', so..."
Krystal: "So who are they talking to then?"
Touré: "Well, they're talking to people who are trained to hate him, who want to hate him, it's a base turn out election so this is how we can rev up the base to work against him."

Wow, Touré is just so smart, isn't he? I never would have figured out that Romney was using coded language about the 'angry black man' unless he used the word 'anger' twice. What a load of crap! Romney wasn't using coded language, he was referencing the whole line of attacks that Obama and his team are using as 'angry'. It had nothing to do with Obama being black, absolutely nothing. And now, Touré is making up new words - 'niggerization' - to help sell his load of crap to the viewing audience.

Krystal, just sitting there going along with what he's saying, then wonders aloud who "they" (I guess Romney and his team) are talking to. Nothing like feeding the race-baiter Touré an easy pitch. He reveals his true thoughts for all to hear: they are talking to people who are *trained to hate him* (him being Obama). Yes, there must be schools out there just training people left and right to hate the President. It's a complete farce, and fortunately the one lone conservative of the bunch has her wits about her and challenges Touré.

Cupp: "Let me get this straight, just so I have this straight. In addition to calling Mitt Romney something of a racist and the whole of the base as racist. Joe Biden makes a racially charged comment, which you and many others on the Left called divisive. Mitt Romney comes out, calls that comment divisive, but because he used the word 'angry', now his is the racially charged comment. Do you see how dishonest that is?"

S.E. Cupp got it right! This is what the Left does - turn things around and calls the Right racists. And Touré didn't just call Romney a racist, he essentially called the entire Republican party racist. He attempts to answer:

Touré: "Well, you know, I didn't call anybody racist, right, because I don't want to deal with that, it's a bit too much..."
Cupp: "Oh, certainly you were implying that Mitt Romney and the base will respond to this dog-whistle, race, racially charged coding...
Touré: "Yes."
Cupp: "...and, hate Obama, 'the angry black man'?"
Touré: "The GOP has been working..."
Cupp: "That is so irresponsible!"
Touré: "The GOP has been working with racial codes going back to Reagan and perhaps before. I mean,

going back to Nixon with the war on drugs, Reagan with the 'welfare queens', ah, the first Bush with the, uh, Willie Horton. I mean this is typical Lee Atwater politics, Karl Rove politics. This is typical Republican playbook."

Cupp: "Again, so then the whole of the party, the whole of the party uses this racial coding?"

Krystal: "He's not saying that."

Cupp: "Oh, he just did!"

Krystal: "He's not saying that, but he is calling out this particular instance."

Touré: "But this is not a revolutionary comment, this is a constituency, all-white party that rejects the black vote..."

Cupp: "You have two white guys in Joe Biden and Mitt Romney. Joe Biden made the overtly racial comment, and has a history of making bigoted remarks. Mitt Romney was responding to that comment, and yet he is the one responsible for whole Republican history of racism, in politics."

Krystal: "But that's not what Touré's saying, you're twisting his words."

Touré: "No, but he's using the playbook that Republican's have been using for decades now, and I was just waiting..."

I realize that this is quite a lot to read, but it's all important. Touré is a race-baiter without question. He's convinced that he can hear racism in practically everything any Republican says. He's sure of it because he's also convinced that people have been trained to hate the President in particular, and black people in general. What's really sad is that, aside from S.E. Cupp challenging him on this, he probably won't get any push-back at all. Even Krystal was trying to defend him, though she was ultimately useless.

One other piece to point out in the video - the one white guy of the foursome, Steve Kornacki, of Salon fame, was notably silent during these 3+ minutes. I'm not sure if he soiled himself as the 'niggerization' accusations flew around, but he got camera time for a couple of seconds and he appeared as though he had just stepped into the Twilight Zone and couldn't believe what he was hearing. It was quite funny!

Desperately Trying
To Find Racism

Date: August 17, 2012

Like so many folks on the Left, if they can't find something to demonize Republicans with, they'll just make things up. Adele Stan at AlterNet.org is no exception. She's brash enough to list out seven ways that Republicans use race to scare white people. Not only that, in her lead up to the list, she claims (without evidence) that Republicans since the beginning of 2012 have been race-baiting. Weakly, she points to Newt Gingrich's 'food stamp President' remark as racist. Why don't we go through a few of these so that we can understand just how foolish Adele and her ilk are.

#1: An Embryo is Just Like An Enslaved Human Being

She starts this point with a pretty shocking title, but that's where it ends. Adele brings out an essay that

Representative Paul Ryan wrote for the Heritage Foundation back in 2010. In it, he argues that the Supreme Court, which is supposed to be the "guardian of rights" for all Americans, got it wrong with their decisions in *Dred Scott vs. Sandford* and *Roe vs. Wade*. Not only did they get it wrong, but Ryan says that they got it SO wrong that they "'disqualified' a whole category of human beings, with profoundly tragic results". Below is what Adele excerpted out from his article:

"...Twice in the past the U.S. Supreme Court—charged with being the guardian of rights—has failed so drastically in making this crucial determination that it "disqualified" a whole category of human beings, with profoundly tragic results.

"The first time was in the 1857 case, Dred Scott v. Sandford. The Court held, absurdly, that Africans and their American descendants, whether slave or free, could not be citizens with a right to go to court to enforce contracts or rights or for any other reason. Why? Because "among the whole human race," the Court declared, "the enslaved African race were not intended to be included...[T]hey had no rights which the white man was bound to respect."..."

"...The second time the Court failed in a case regarding the definition of "human" was in Roe v. Wade in 1973, when the Supreme Court made virtually the identical mistake. At what point in time does a human being exist, the state of Texas asked. The Court refused to answer..."

"Since the Court decided there was no "consensus" on when fetuses become human persons, it struck down abortion restrictions in all 50 states that thought they had reached a "consensus." ... The Court did not say that, given the lack of consensus, the matter ought to be left to the states. It did not choose to err on the side of caution, since human lives might be at stake. Nor did it choose not to rule on the matter. These options would seem to be rational courses in light of the Court's stated agnosticism..."

If you were to take her excerpts without looking at the rest of the article, I could see where you might come to the same conclusions that Adele did. However, *I did* read the rest of the article, and I found that she cherry-picked passages that would make it appear as though her conclusions are correct. Let's look at everything, including (and I might add, *especially*) the parts that she left out:

"The car which I exercised my freedom of choice to purchase is not such an entity and does not "qualify" for protection of human rights. I can drive it, lend it, kick it, sell it, or junk it, at will. On the other hand, the widow who lives next door does "qualify" as a person, and the government must secure her human rights, which cannot be abandoned to anyone's arbitrary will.

"Yet, identifying who "qualifies" as a human being has historically proved to be more difficult than the above examples suggest. Twice in the past the U.S. Supreme Court—charged with being the guardian of rights—has failed so drastically in making this crucial determination that it "disqualified" a whole category of human beings, with profoundly tragic results.

"The first time was in the 1857 case, Dred Scott v. Sandford. The Court held, absurdly, that Africans and their American descendants, whether slave or free, could not be citizens with a right to go to court to enforce contracts or rights or for any other reason.

Why? Because "among the whole human race," the Court declared, "the enslaved African race were not intended to be included...[T]hey had no rights which the white man was bound to respect." In other words, persons of African origin did not "qualify" as human beings for purposes of protecting their natural rights. It was held that, since the white man did not recognize them as having such rights, they didn't have them. The implication was that Africans were property—things that white persons could choose to buy and sell. In contrast, whites did "qualify," so government protected their natural rights.

"Every person in this country was wounded the day this dreadful opinion was handed down by this nation's highest tribunal. It made a mockery of the American idea that human equality and rights were given by God and recognized by government, not constructed by governments or ethnic groups by consensus vote. The abhorrent decision directly led to terrible bloodshed and opened up a racial gap that has never been completely overcome. The second time the Court failed in a case regarding the definition of "human" was in Roe v. Wade in 1973, when the Supreme Court made virtually the identical mistake. At what point in time does a human being exist, the state of Texas asked. The Court refused to answer: "We need not resolve the difficult question of when life begins. When those trained in the respective disciplines of medicine, philosophy, and theology are unable to arrive at any consensus, the judiciary, at this point in the development of man's knowledge, is not in a position to speculate as to the answer." In other words, the Court would not "qualify" unborn children as living persons whose human rights must be guaranteed.

"Since the Court decided there was no "consensus" on when fetuses become human persons, it struck down abortion restrictions in all 50 states that thought they had reached a "consensus." Only those already born "qualified" for protection. Moreover, the already born were empowered to deny, at will, the rights of persons still in the womb. The Court did not say that, given the lack of consensus, the matter ought to be left to the states. It did not choose to err on the side of caution, since human lives might be at stake. Nor did it choose not to rule on the matter. These options would seem to be rational courses in light of the Court's stated agnosticism. Instead, the Court used the lack of consensus to justify prohibiting states from protecting the life of the unborn."

As you can see, Paul Ryan is not equating a fetus to a slave. What he's doing is explaining in each Supreme Court case how the common sense approach to who is a person, and by extension who deserves protections afford to persons, was turned upside down. She's trying to turn Paul Ryan into a racist, but fails by simply reading his own words. This is Adele manufacturing an issue where none exists.

#2: Allen West - Obama wants to enslave everybody

Adele says that when Representative Allen West was at a campaign rally in his district, he was "throwing down on the language of bondage". Here is what he said:

West: "He (Obama) does not want you to have the self-esteem of getting up and earning and having that title of American. He'd rather you be his slave."

Unfortunately, what Adele is guilty of here is the sin of omission. She omitted a large portion of West's speech that came before that small part she took out of context. Here is the full piece of what he said:

West: "This is not about party. It is about principle. This is about understanding one of those principles. This is about understanding what limited government really is, and what fiscal responsibility is. My mother taught me a very simple lesson. She said self-esteem comes from doing esteemable things. Sitting at home and getting a check from the government is not going to help your self-esteem. What it will do is make you an *economic* slave to a bunch of people in a far, far distant place.

"This country was established believing in the individual, their sovereignty, their rights, their freedom. Not collective subjugation. Not this...emphasis on dividing us based on race and gender, socioeconomic status or whatever they can try to find up, just so they can retain power over each and every one of us.

"Unfortunately we have a President that has a sign up that says America's not open for business because of his tax policies. Obviously he does not understand that small business owners operate from their personal income tax rate. So do you want to raise those personal income tax rates, top bracket from thirty-three percent up to thirty-seven percent. From thirty-five percent to thirty-nine point six percent. You're talking about affecting the very people that are the economic engine of this country. Why? It's very simple. He does not want you to have the self-esteem of getting up and earning and having that title of American. He'd rather you be his slave, and be economically dependent on him." (emphasis added)

In that piece, West is obviously referring to economic slavery - keeping people down by making them poor and dependent. The other thing that's funny? Allen West is black. I'm POSITIVE that he wasn't using the word 'slave' in the sense that Adele would like to have you believe he is.

#3: Rand Paul - Healthcare reform supporters are slavery promoters

On this one, Adele actually gets the description right with her title. However, it's not as racial as she would like to have you believe. Here is what she highlighted from Andrew Malcolm's post on the *Los Angeles Times* website:

"With regard to the idea of whether you have a right to healthcare, you have to realize what that implies. It's not an abstraction. I'm a physician. That means you have a right to come to my house and conscript me," Paul said recently in a Senate subcommittee hearing.

"It means you believe in slavery. It means that you're going to enslave not only me, but the janitor at my hospital, the person who cleans my office, the assistants who work in my office, the nurses," Paul said, adding that there is "an implied use of force."

Senator Rand Paul is correct. By saying that you have a right to healthcare, that means that you are essentially turning a physician, a nurse, a nurse practitioner, etc. into your own personal healthcare slave. You are forcing them to do something for you, which is exactly what slavery in this country was -

forcing someone else (a black person), against their will, to do something for you (the slave owner). Does this make Rand Paul a racist? Hardly! He is using a very logical and appropriate comparison to illustrate exactly what supporters of the "right to healthcare" are asking for. Adele simply has her race glasses on and is seeing racism where none exists.

#4: Michele Bachmann: Healthcare reform and the national debt are forms of slavery

Here Adele is trying to do two things. First, she's trying a second time to claim that any mention of slavery when it comes to the ACA is just racial in nature (she failed the first time with Rand Paul above, and she fails again here for the same reasons). Second, Adele tries to claim that Michele Bachmann is using racial language when she (Bachmann) compares being in debt to slavery. Here again she's wrong.

Why is she wrong on Bachmann? It becomes obvious when one thinks about it for a bit. Let's say that you wanted $10,000 and I had the funds to loan you. We agree to do so, and you are now in debt to me for the $10,000, plus interest. What you have now done is tied your hands by agreeing to take the loan; you've put yourself into slavery, in a sense. I say this because you no longer have the freedom to do what you want, when you want. You have obligated yourself to making payments to me over the course of time, and that means that you no longer have as much financial freedom to do what you want. There is a certain amount of money that you must allocate on a monthly basis to pay me. On top of that, you have obligated yourself to actually paying MORE than the $10,000 that you were loaned because of the interest that I am charging you for using some of my property (that's what money is - property). Until you pay off that loan, it will be hanging over your head, reminding you that you must continue to work and pay it. You can't just not pay it either, because I have the law on my side and the contract will be enforced and you will still end up paying it off.

If you don't want to have your hands tied in this way, don't take out a loan. If you can't afford something at the time, odds are you will do just fine without it until such time as you can pay for it fully in cash rather than take out a loan. Again, this has nothing to do with race, but everything to do with common sense and making responsible choices.

#5: Rick Santorum and Michele Bachmann: Slavery was good for the black family

This is a pretty bold statement, to insinuate that these two people agree with the notion that slavery was good for black people. Where did Adele get this idea? From this statement that appeared in a pledge that they both signed that was put out by the *FAMiLY Leader*:

"Slavery had a disastrous impact on African-American families, yet sadly a child born into slavery in 1860 was more likely to be raised by his mother and father in a two-parent household than was an African-American baby born after the election of the USA's first African-American President."

Now, there are a number of unfortunate things here, not the least of which is that no statistics were provided (that I'm aware of) to support such a claim like what *FAMiLY Leader* had put in their pledge. But, for the sake of argument, let's say that it was true and black children born into slavery had the benefit of having both a mother and a father, and that this happened to a higher percentage of black children then as opposed to now. Would that be a racist statement or comment? No, absolutely not, because it would be a stating of fact, not an emotional opinion.

This statement from the *FAMiLY Leader* immediately states that slavery "had a disastrous impact on African-American families...", and they are right in stating this. But does the rest of the statement, even if it's false, mean that people, and specifically Santorum and Bachmann, are in favor of slavery? Hardly! What Adele does here is twist words to make it seem as though these two politicians are racist, when in fact they are not and the statement in the pledge by *FAMiLY Leader* is not. This is race-baiting at it's finest.

#6: Herman Cain: U.S. tax code = slavery

Here again the use of the word "slave" in any context immediately means the person using it is a racist. Here's a partial transcript of a Herman Cain for President ad that Adele references to prove her point:

"Our tax code is the 21st-century version of slavery. The IRS has become the overseer of the American people. In a Herman Cain administration, April 15th will no longer be a day to be dreaded. My 9-9-9 economic growth and jobs plan is a major step towards tearing the chains off the backs of the American people... We'll all be able to say, 'Free at last! Free at last!'....."

Herman knows, and many other Americans know, what the IRS is like, and it's not a fuzzy, cuddly teddy bear. What he means is that the tax code is so onerous, so convoluted, so difficult, that individuals and businesses must plan their lives around how certain decisions will affect them and the taxes that they pay.

IRS agents have gained a reputation as being vicious and tenacious, even when they are wrong. The tax code is akin to slavery in that it keeps people down and prevents them from choosing their own destiny.

Herman Cain wanted to make the tax code much simpler to comply with, much easier to understand. In doing so, people would then be free to live the American dream by pursuing what they consider to be their happiness, whatever that is. Herman wanted to alleviate the oppression and to have people stop feeling like they were prisoners. He's not racist at all - pretty hard to be racist when you're black like Herman Cain!

#7: Rick Perry: The government is Pharaoh, and citizens, the slaves

Like some of the other points Adele tries to make, this one she figures is obvious enough that all she needs to do is simply introduce the statement and then the readers will see just how blatantly racist it is. Here's what Rick Perry said in an interview:

"I think we're going through those difficult economic times for a purpose, to bring us back to those Biblical principles of ... not spending all of our money, not asking for Pharaoh to give everything to everybody and to take care of folks, because at the end of the day, it's slavery. And we become slaves to government."

Slaves to government. What Perry means is that, as we ask government to do more and more for us, things that we can and should do ourselves, the government needs more and more of our resources, our property, in order to make that happen. As such, we then become slaves to the government because we owe so much to the government in order that they provide so much to us. In short, it means that we no longer have the freedom to choose how to spend our money, our property, because we have turned that over to the government. It's freedom FROM choice, not freedom OF choice.

Adele doesn't like the slavery references that these folks, and others, use. Many times, and these examples are cases of this, the word is used correctly and the meaning that comes with it helps to paint an all-too-clear picture. When used in this manner, the word slavery or slave is appropriate and not at all racist. But for so many on the Left, Adele included, any mention of the word is code language for racist; she and others like her don't even bother to understand the meaning that is trying to be conveyed, they only jump to racist conclusions.

Reporter Who Interrupts Obama At Press Conference...Is Racist?

Date: June 15, 2012

President Obama held a press conference outside the White House in the Rose Garden on the topic of immigration, and there was a reporter, Neil Munro, from *The Daily Caller* that appeared intent on interrupting the President in order to ask his question(s) and put the President on the spot. Supposedly, one could argue that this reporter's cause was helped because there were live cameras broadcasting the event, so he could make a spectacle out of things. The essence of the reporter's question was to ask why the President would want to provide amnesty for up to a million illegal immigrants when the unemployment rate was so high.

Now, I'm sure we can all agree that the timing wasn't appropriate. However, Neil himself provided the reasoning behind his actions when he appeared on Sean Hannity's FoxNews television show, *Hannity*, the following Monday, June 18. In that interview, Neil claimed that he thought the President was nearly finished with his remarks, and that knowing how Presidents are, figured that he would try to get in a question just before the President finished speaking. Now, this does sound a bit far-fetched, but Hannity was ready to jump to Neil's defense by showing a video clip of one Sam Donaldson, then a reporter for ABC News, doing practically the same thing to President Reagan.

This probably would be the end of it, if not for Touré of MNBC fame. The co-host of the show *The Cycle* claimed, while serving as a guest on another MSNBC show, that the cause of the incident was because of racism:

Touré: "I-I wonder how strategic it was, if he went to this saying 'I'm going to interrupt the President in this way.'. Some people will say that what I'm about to say is not part of this and your crazy for bringing this up. Some people are saying 'Well of course it's part of this.'. But this disrespect of this human being is - cannot be disconnected from the fact that he's black."

He continued his explanation:

Touré: "There is a basic, lesser humanity generally ascribed to black people, even one this alpha, this much in power, this much in control, and that you would have people like a Joe Wilson, like a..."

And continued further:

Touré: "Or just for white people to see a black person in power, and just say 'I don't have to respect you.'. And even at the point of decorum when he says 'I'm speaking, I have acknowledged you, rude person, but we are doing this thing together, and I'm still talking.'..."

At this point in the book, I'm sure you can see how Touré basically sees everything as racism, and this incident is no different. Basically, he's made up his mind that Neil didn't interrupt the President for any reason OTHER than because he's a racist and wanted to attempt to make the President look bad.

Also, who in this country ascribes a 'lesser humanity' to black people, as Touré implies? This is nothing more than him saying that, pretty much, the entirety of white America views black people, and this President, as less human or not as important. The sheer audacity of this man is incredible! Where does he get off saying things like this? And why aren't the other people on the show even trying to call him on this? Once again, liberals like Touré have created controversy where there was none, all so that they can continue hammering on the narrative that conservatives, or in this case anyone who interrupts the President, are racist.

Yahoo! News Chief Reveals His True Beliefs

Date: August 29, 2012

ABC News was streaming a live webcast in connection with the Republican National Convention held in Tampa, Florida, when people watching and listening could hear words that would shock and surprise them. What were they and who said it? Here's the first answer:

"They're not concerned at all. They're happy to have a party with *black people drowning*." (emphasis added)

The person who said that was referencing the fact that the GOP convention was still going forward despite the fact that hurricane Issac was predicted to make landfall somewhere around New Orleans. Who said this despicable thing? David Chalian, the *former* Washington bureau chief of Yahoo! News. I emphasized *former* because in very swift action, Yahoo! News fired him for his obviously racial comments. Yahoo! News should be commended for taking appropriate action that sends a clear signal.

While this comment could seem out of place and, to some, even innocuous, it's actually indicative of many in the wider media arena. As shown in previous events early in the book, there are many media people, and others, who would agree with David's remark. It's a deeply offensive remark, both for black people and white people. It's offensive to black people because it assumes that they are helpless and forgotten, which is definitely not the case. It's offensive to white people because it assumes that the storm would only be hitting places where black people live, and we know that's also not the case. This statement is just wrong on so many levels, and reveals much about the speaker himself. A true race-baiter.

Conclusions

As I stated at the very beginning of this book, I got tired of hearing things like what I've outlined in this book. I wrote this book to help get people to pay more attention to what is going on with our media, with our politicians, and with others who are reporting on our political system in this country. Too many people have an ax to grind, and they are choosing to grind it on conservatives. If they can't find something, they'll just make it up. And unfortunately, too many people are taking what they are fed and believing it.

These are just the most egregious, over-the-top examples, yet there are countless others out there that could be delved into. Do a Google Alert for yourself on "race" or "race baiting" and see what gets to your inbox each day. It's astounding! I'm doing what I can to educate people, as that's the first step in getting things changed. Listen, really listen, to what these folks are saying. Then start researching some of these things for yourself. The media and others are betting that you won't do the research, so you have to prove them wrong and show them that you aren't the idiot they take you for.

What else can you do? You can help by calling these people on it when they say dumb things that are plainly, obviously racial in nature. Email them, post on forums, blogs, etc., don't watch their shows or read their articles. And let others know to do the same - your neighbors, friends, family and others. Take opportunities as they present themselves to try educating your fellow Americans. And lastly, share this book with people so that they can really see what's going on with the Left and the media. These people need to be shunned and shamed into thinking before they speak/write/act. End the moronic race-baiting and help the country move into better times.

Thank you for reading this book, and for caring about our country!

References

NOTE - These website links were tested and active between September 16 and September 19. By the time you read this book, these links may no longer be functional/active.

Part 1:

Anderson, Jennifer. "Schools beat the drum for equity". *portlandtribune.com*. 5 September 2012. Web. 18 September 2012. <http://portlandtribune.com/pt-rss/9-news/114604-schools-beat-the-drum-for-equity>

Falkenberg, Lisa. "Romney at NAACP: An impossible crowd". *chron.com*. 11 July 2012. Web. 17 September 2012. <http://www.chron.com/news/falkenberg/article/Romney-at-NAACP-An-impossible-crowd-3700383.php>

Malkin, Michelle. "The Condensed Liberal Handbook of Racial Code Words". *michellemalkin.com*. 31

August 2012. Web. 16 September 2012.
<http://michellemalkin.com/2012/08/31/the-condensed-liberal-handbook-of-racial-code-words/>

Robinson, John. "Diversity Notes". State Magazine July/August 2012: page 8. Print.
<http://www.state.gov/documents/organization/195572.pdf>

Schwartz, Ian. "McConnell Saying Obama Wants to be in PGA is Racist (video)". *realclearpolitics.com*. 29 August 2012. Web. 17 September 2012.
<http://www.realclearpolitics.com/video/2012/08/29/msnbc_mitch_mcconnell_saying_obama_wants_to_be_in_pga_is_racist.html>

Schwartz, Ian. "Perry Calling Obama 'Privileged' is 'Dog Whistle' to Racists". *realclearpolitics.com*. 17 November 2011. Web. 18 September 2012.
<http://www.realclearpolitics.com/video/2011/11/17/washington_posts_capehart_perry_calling_obama_privileged_is_racist.html>

Schwartz, Ian. "Racist to Say Food Stamp Refers to Black (video)". *realclearpolitics.com*. 27 August 2012. Web. 17 September 2012.
<http://www.realclearpolitics.com/video/2012/08/27/gingrich_to_chris_matthews_racist_to_say_food_stamp_refers_to_black.html>

Smilke, Basil. "Basil Smilke on Racial Code Words in Election Coverage (video)". *ovguide.com*. n.d. Web. 16 September 2012.
<http://www.ovguide.com/video/basil-smikle-on-racial-code-words-in-election-coverage-922ca39ce10036ba0e11ae82c5eb6a21>

Spierling, Charlie. "Romney NAACP speech part of 'racist' southern strategy". *washingtonexaminer.com*. 12 July 2012. Web. 17 September 2012. <http://washingtonexaminer.com/msnbc-romney-naacp-speech-part-of-racist-southern-strategy/article/2501948#.UFfdDq6ca_I>

Stripling, Jack. "Professor in Chief". *insidehighered.com*. 10 February 2010. Web. 18 September 2012. <http://www.insidehighered.com/news/2010/02/10/obama>

Tomasky, Michael. "Michael Tomasky on Mitt Romney the Race Baiter at the NAACP". *thedailybeast.com*. 12 July 2012. Web. 18 September 2012. <http://www.thedailybeast.com/articles/2012/07/12/michael-tomasky-on-mitt-romney-the-race-baiter-at-the-naacp.html>

Touré. "How to Read Political Racial Code". *ideas.time.com*. 6 September 2012. Web. 18 September 2012. <http://ideas.time.com/2012/09/06/how-to-read-political-racial-code/>

Williams, Juan. "Racial code words obscure real issues". *thehill.com*. 30 January 2012. Web. 16 September 2012. <http://thehill.com/opinion/columnists/juan-williams/207295-2012-racial-code-words-obscure-real-issue>

Part 2:

ABC News. "GOP Rep. to Obama: 'You Lie!'". *ABC News*. YouTube, 9 September 2009. Web. 19 September 2012. <http://www.youtube.com/watch?v=qgce06Yw2ro>

Byers, Dylan. "Yahoo News Fires David Chalian". *politico.com*. 29 August 2012. Web. 19 September 2012. <http://www.politico.com/blogs/media/2012/08/yahoo-news-fires-david-chalian-source-133662.html>

Chait, Jonathan. "The Real Reason 'You Didn't Build That' Works". *nymag.com*. 27 July 2012. Web. 19 September 2012. <http://nymag.com/daily/intel/2012/07/real-reason-you-didnt-build-that-works.html>

Christopher, Tommy. "Mitt Romney's 'Obama Isn't Working' Banner Evokes Racial Stereotypes". *mediaite.com*. 19 April 2012. Web. 19 September 2012. <http://www.mediaite.com/online/mitt-romneys-obama-isnt-working-banner-evokes-racial-stereotypes/>

Contee, Cheryl. "Romney's Race-Baiting Welfare Ad Divides to Conquer Working Class Whites". *jackandjillpolitics.com*. 8 August 2012. Web. 19 September 2012. <http://www.jackandjillpolitics.com/2012/08/romneys-race-baiting-welfare-ad-divides-to-conquer-working-class-whites/>

Darcy, Oliver. "University Sponsors Campaign to Undermine 'White Privilege'". *d-umn.campusreform.org*. 21 June 2012. Web. 19

September 2012. <http://d-umn.campusreform.org/school/blog/?ID=3059>

Dowd, Maureen. "Boy, Oh, Boy". *nytimes.com*. 12 September 2009. Web. 19 September 2012. <http://www.nytimes.com/2009/09/13/opinion/13dowd.html?_r=1>

Drennen, Kyle. "ObamaCare Protestors 'Racist', Including Black Gun-Owner". *newsbusters.org*. 18 August 2009. Web. 18 September 2012. <http://newsbusters.org/blogs/kyle-drennen/2009/08/18/msnbc-obamacare-protesters-racist-including-black-gun-owner>

"'Hardball with Chris Matthews' for Monday, April 23, 2012". *msnbc.msn.com*. 9 May 2012. Web. 18 September 2012. <http://www.msnbc.msn.com/id/47356764/ns/msnbc-hardball_with_chris_matthews/#.UBQjM6Cca_I>

Holt, Mytheos. "How To Tell Which Ads Are 'Racist': Newspaper Pens Unbelievable Litmus Test". *theblaze.com*. 26 July 2012. Web. 18 September 2012. <http://www.theblaze.com/stories/how-to-tell-which-ads-are-racist-newspaper-pens-unbelievable-litmus-test/>

Huston, Warner Todd. "Response To Colorado Shooting All About Racism". *breitbart.com*. 25 July 2012. Web. 18 September 2012. <http://www.breitbart.com/Big-Journalism/2012/07/24/MSNBC-s-Toure-Colorado-Shooting-All-About-Racism>

Kirell, Andrew. "MSNBC's Touré: Romney Engaging

In The 'Niggerization' Of Obama". *mediaite.com*. 16
August 2012. Web. 19 September 2012.
<http://www.mediaite.com/tv/msnbcs-toure-to-panel-
romney-engaging-in-the-niggerization-of-obama/>

"Maxine Waters plays the race card, smears Tea Party at
Sunday church service". *therightscoop.com*. 23 May
2012. Web. 19 September 2012.
<http://www.therightscoop.com/maxine-waters-plays-
the-race-card-smears-tea-party-at-sunday-church-
service/>

McIlwain, Charlton and Caliendo, Stephen. "Is a pro-
Romney ad racist? Five questions to ask yourself".
csmonitor.com. 23 July 2012. Web. 19 September
2012.
<http://www.csmonitor.com/Commentary/2012/0723/Is-
a-pro-Romney-ad-racist-Five-questions-to-ask-
yourself/Does-the-ad-reference-racial-stereotypes>

MichaelSavage4Prez. "Allen West - Obama Wants
Americans To 'Be His Slave' - (7/1/12)".
MichaelSavage4Prez's channel. YouTube, 2 July 2012.
Web. 19 September 2012.
<http://www.youtube.com/watch?v=bcvQdChNaII>

mittromney. "Right Choice". *mittromney's channel*.
YouTube, 7 August 2012. Web. 19 September 2012.
<http://www.youtube.com/watch?v=0F4LtTlktm0>

mittromney. "Shame On You". *mittromney's channel*.
YouTube, 29 June 2012. Web. 19 September 2012.
<http://www.youtube.com/watch?v=sxoVqMhuzTo>

Negrin, Matt. "Romney Says He Knew He'd Be Booed
at NAACP". *abcnews.go.com*. 11 July 2012. Web. 19

September 2012.
<http://abcnews.go.com/Politics/OTUS/romney-says-he-expected-to-be-booed-at-naacp/story?
id=16753886#.UFp5bK6ca_J>

NewsPoliticsNow. "Reporter Who Interrupted Obama Defends Himself On Hannity". *newspoliticsnow's channel*. YouTube, 18 June 2012. Web. 19 September 2012. <http://www.youtube.com/watch?
v=YYAOm8LvqlI&feature=related>

Nolte, John. "NY Mag: Hitting Obama For 'You Didn't Build That' is Racist" *breitbart.com*. 27 July 2012. Web. 19 September 2012.
<http://www.breitbart.com/Big-Journalism/2012/07/27/You-Didnt-Build-That-Is-Racist>

Nolte, John. "Yahoo's Chalian on ABC Webcast: Romney's 'Happy To Have A Party When Black People Drown'". *breitbart.com*. 29 August 2012. Web. 19 September 2012. <http://www.breitbart.com/Big-Journalism/2012/08/29/Shock-ABC-News-Romneys-Party-As-Black-People-Die>

obamaisntworking.com. n.d. Web. 19 September 2012. <http://www.obamaisntworking.com/>

Pavlich, Katie. "MSNBC Host Jumps The Shark, Tries To Make Colorado About Race". *townhall.com*. 25 July 2012. Web. 18 September 2012.
<http://townhall.com/tipsheet/katiepavlich/2012/07/25/msnbc_host_jumps_the_shark_tries_to_make_colorado_about_race>

Pavlich, Katie. "MSNBC Host: Romney Wanted to

Prove he Knew How to Talk Down to Black People".
townhall.com. 13 July 2012. Web. 19 September 2012.
<http://townhall.com/tipsheet/katiepavlich/2012/07/13/m
snbc_host_romney_wanted_to_prove_he_knew_how_to
_talk_down_to_black_people>

Pavlich, Katie. "Romney Receives Standing Ovation for
Straight Talk at NAACP Convention". *townhall.com*.
11 July 2012. Web. 19 September 2012.
<http://townhall.com/tipsheet/katiepavlich/2012/07/11/r
omney_receives_standing_ovation_for_straight_talk_at_
naacp_convention>

Poor, Jeff and May, Caroline. "Bill Maher finds six
black men to deem Drudge racist". *dailycaller.com*. 16
June 2012. Web. 19 September 2012.
<http://dailycaller.com/2012/06/16/bill-maher-finds-six-
black-men-to-deem-matt-drudge-racist-video/>

Rector, Robert and Grossman, Andrew. "HHS Can't
Waive Workfare". *heritage.org*. 9 August 2012. Web.
19 September 2012.
<http://www.heritage.org/research/commentary/2012/08/
hhs-cannot-waive-workfare>

Ryan, Paul. "The Cause of Life Can't be Severed From
the Cause of Freedom". *paulryan.house.gov*. 20
September 2010. Web. 19 September 2012.
<http://paulryan.house.gov/news/documentsingle.aspx?
DocumentID=207539>

Schwartz, Ian. "Obama Heckling Can't 'Be
Disconnected From' His Race". *realclearpolitics.com*.
15 June 2012. Web. 19 September 2012.
<http://www.realclearpolitics.com/video/2012/06/15/tou
re_obama_heckling_cant_be_disconnected_from_the_fa

ct_that_hes_black.html>

Shapiro, Rebecca. "Chris Matthews Calls Republican Party 'Grand Wizard Crowd'". *huffingtonpost.com*. 24 April 2012. Web. 18 September 2012. <http://www.huffingtonpost.com/2012/04/24/chris-matthews-grand-wizard-republican-party_n_1448379.html>

Stan, Adele. "7 Ways Republicans Use Slavery Rhetoric to Scare White People". *alternet.org*. 17 August 2012. Web. 19 September 2012. <http://www.alternet.org/election-2012/7-ways-republicans-use-slavery-rhetoric-scare-white-people?paging=off>

Theguardianpost2. "Liberal Trash Ed Schultz Get's caught". *theguardianpost2's channel*. YouTube, 17 August 2011. Web. 18 September 2012. <http://www.youtube.com/watch?v=1wr1yzfHcls>

Tyrone. "NBC and ABC's race baiting Journalism EXPOSED Part 1". *Wake Up Black America*. Blogger.com. 3 April 2012. Web. 18 September 2012. <http://wakeupblackamerica.blogspot.com/2012/04/nbc-and-abcs-race-baiting-journalism.html>

Unfaircampaign.org. n.d. Web. 19 September 2012. <http://unfaircampaign.org/>

Vozzella, Laura. "Va. state senator blames racism for Romney gains". *washingtonpost.com*. 24 July 2012. Web. 18 September 2012. <http://www.washingtonpost.com/blogs/virginia-politics/post/va-state-senator-blames-racism-for-romney-gains/2012/07/24/gJQAArsQ7W_blog.html>